THE ZONE OF INTEREST

A Cinematic Exploration of the Holocaust

JOHN CLEAN

Copyright © by John Clean 2024.
All rights reserved.

Before this document is duplicated or reproduced in any manner, the publisher's consent must be gained. Therefore, the contents within can neither be stored electronically, transferred, nor kept in a database. Neither in Part nor full can the document be copied, scanned, faxed, or retained without approval from the publisher or creator.

Table of Contents

INTRODUCTION

CHAPTER 1

CHAPTER 2

CHAPTER 3

CONCLUSION

Introduction

The Zone of Interest, a historical drama based on Martin Amis' 2014 book, will be released in UK theaters on February 2nd, 2024. The film looks at the ethically complex environment of the Auschwitz concentration camp through the perspective of its commander, Rudolf Höss, and his family. The film creates a disturbing portrayal of life in the shadow of unspeakable misery, compelling us to confront the intricacies of human behavior and the decisions people make in the face of enormous evil.

To completely grasp the film's effect, one must first understand the Holocaust and the importance of Auschwitz. The film is directed by Jonathan Glazer, a critically renowned director recognized for his visually spectacular and psychologically challenging films. The brilliant ensemble, led by German actor Christian Friedel and Austrian actress Sandra Hüller, conveys the intricacies and complexity of people navigating a terrifying reality.

The Zone of Interest is a difficult film to watch because it confronts viewers with painful realities and compels them to consider the distinctions between good and evil, normality and monster. By confronting these facts, the film finally forces us to consider our own obligations and the risks of complacency in the face of injustice.

Chapter 1

Plot Summary

The Zone of Interest is a frightening Holocaust film made by Jonathan Glazer that examines the dynamics of genocide in a new and unnerving way. The film opens with a beautiful picture of a family picnicking by a river, but the family's car's number plate is found to bore the emblem of the SS, the Nazi regime's elite guard. The video then cuts to the current day, when cleaners scrupulously maintain the Auschwitz Memorial Museum, highlighting the compartmentalization of misery. The film's visual narrative, such as the use of pulsing orange-red light from the crematoria and the metaphorical link between a children's pool and the camp's gas chambers, is both horrific and thought-provoking. Unlike classic Holocaust accounts, The Zone of Interest depicts the Nazis as average people tending to their gardens and going about their everyday lives, with the tragedies of the camp serving as a terrifying background. The film, which stars Sandra Hüller, Christian Friedel, Ralph Herforth, Max Beck, and Lilli Falk, will be released in UK theaters on February 2, 2024.

Genre and Themes

The Zone of Interest is a gripping drama directed by Jonathan Glazer on the Holocaust crimes. The film, slated to be released on February 2, 2024, combines drama, history, and battle. It presents Nazis as average people going about their everyday lives, with the horrors of the concentration camp serving as a frightening background. The video stresses the normality of evil and the banality of genocide, as well as the compartmentalization of pain via walls, borders, and geographical distance.

The film's central themes include the banality of evil, the compartmentalization of pain, and the disturbing closeness of a family's peaceful lives to the horrors of a concentration camp. The film's visual narrative, which incorporates symbolic links and eerie themes, provides a riveting examination of the Holocaust and the human propensity for atrocities.

To summarize, The Zone of Interest is a thought-provoking and artistically spectacular picture that expertly navigates the complexity of its genre and topics. Its distinct approach to narrative and visual symbolism makes it an important and striking contribution to the cinematic scene.

Chapter 2

Character Analysis

The Zone of Interest is a thought-provoking story set at the Auschwitz concentration camp, following the lives of three people, Angelus Thomsen, Paul Doll, and Szmul Zacharias, who were all severely impacted by the Nazi war machine and the Holocaust. Thomsen's story emphasizes the difficulties of sustaining personal connections in the face of war and cruelty, while Doll struggles with the moral implications of his position of leadership inside the camp. His depiction of envy and retribution is a sobering reminder of the depths to which people can go when consumed by hate, as well as the tragic implications of individual acts in the context of genocide.

Zacharias' viewpoint provides a unique perspective, depicting the confusion and despair inside the camp as the tide swings against the Nazis. His experiences, along with those of the inmates and guards, serve as a harsh reminder of the Nazis' approaching defeat and the far-reaching consequences of this change in power relations inside the camps.

The film's adaptation of Martin Amis' book, together with Jonathan Glazer's directorial choices, provide a riveting and extremely frightening investigation of the Holocaust, depicting the tragedy from the perspectives of both perpetrators and victims. The characters are effective vehicles for delving into the varied nature of the Holocaust and its long-lasting repercussions.

Cinematography and Visuals

Jonathan Glazer's artistically stunning film The Zone of Interest portrays the Holocaust in a terrifying and horrifying way. The film employs avant-garde methods and cinematography, with Lukasz Zal's goal being to provide unappealing, objective visuals free of emotional manipulation. Sony Venice cameras provide crisp, high-contrast photos that showcase personalities in a simple, almost documentary-style. AI, infrared photography, and ambitious approaches to fully immerse the spectator in the horrific narrative of the

Holocaust define the visual design. The purposeful and uncomfortable decision made in the film to depict Auschwitz commander Rudolf Höss and his wife Hedwig emphasizes the banality of evil and the readiness to accept it. The Zone of Interest is a thought-provoking examination of the human propensity for atrocity and the lasting impact of this terrible chapter in history. The visual storytelling in the film effectively conveys the deep and horrific nature of the subject.

Chapter 3

Impact and Reception

The controversial film The Zone of Interest, directed by Jonathan Glazer, has prompted arguments regarding its influence on historical and cultural portrayal. The film, which will be released on February 2, 2024, has been lauded for its unusual and frightening portrayal of the Holocaust. Critics have commended the film's use of cutting-edge methods like artificial intelligence and infrared photography to express the story's deep and frightening nature. However, some reviewers have questioned the film's goal and courage to tackle the atrocities of the Holocaust. The film's purposeful focus on the banalities of the individuals' existence in the camp has sparked debate, with some claiming that the film's perceived ordinariness detracts from the severity of the subject matter.

In terms of historical and cultural depiction, The Zone of Interest has been lauded as a "breathtaking masterpiece" and a "monumental cinematic achievement," delivering a fascinating and profoundly unsettling investigation of the Holocaust. The film's relevance stems from its capacity to tackle genocide methods and the long-term consequences of this terrible period in history. By portraying the Nazis as everyday people, the film emphasizes the unnerving normality of evil and the readiness to accept it, pushing viewers to confront the horrors of the Holocaust.

Conclusion

The Zone of Interest is a frightening and thought-provoking film made by Jonathan Glazer that depicts the Holocaust in an unusual and horrific way. The film uses unique methods to express the narrative's deep and frightening nature, highlighting the banality of evil and the willingness to accept it. The film's purposeful visual design and technical technology immerse the spectator in the disturbing story, providing a thought-provoking examination of the human propensity for cruelty. Despite its mixed critical reaction, the film's value stems from its ability to face the dynamics of genocide and provide a fascinating and highly disturbing analysis of the Holocaust. The Zone of Interest is a magnificent masterwork that finds its strength in what is unseen, surveying the destruction of the Holocaust from an emotionally horrific standpoint. Its creative and original methodology, paired with its somber subject matter, results in a thought-provoking and frightening experience that is highly recommended for anyone interested in delving into the nuances of human behavior and the Holocaust's lasting impact.

The Zone of Interest foregoes a standard story structure in favor of a collection of evocative vignettes that connect the lives of numerous persons living under the terrible tragedy of Auschwitz. While not directly depicted, the concentration camp's presence is palpable throughout the film, with horrors conveyed via sights, sounds, and people' emotions.

Rudolf Höss (Christian Friedel) is the Commandant of Auschwitz, and he lives an apparently ideal family life just outside the camp gates. The video delves into his everyday routines and relationships, contrasting them with the terrible reality he overlooks.

Thomas Wünsche (Götz Schubert): A young SS officer entrusted with supervising the building of a new crematorium, he has a slow moral awakening as he realizes the actual nature of his employment.

Szmul Zacharias (Piotr Nerowski): A Jewish Sonderkommando compelled to work in the crematoria, he stands as a mute witness to the camp's atrocities, symbolizing the victims and emphasizing the dehumanization they experienced.

The film avoids simple explanations and dramatic climaxes by interweaving various storylines. Instead, it asks viewers to confront the disturbing regularity of life for both offenders and victims in the presence of unfathomable cruelty.

Key themes include complicity, ignorance, and the banality of evil.

The Zone of Interest digs into the intricacies of human behavior under severe conditions, examining numerous fundamental themes:

Complicity: Beyond depicting active perpetrators, the film investigates the different types of complicity, both purposeful and passive, that permitted the Holocaust. It questions how apparently regular people may become cogs in a machine of inconceivable evil, pushing spectators to contemplate their own potential for collaboration in unjust institutions.

Ignorance: The film investigates the degree to which conscious or inadvertent ignorance enabled the Holocaust. While some individuals seem to be completely unconscious of the scale of the horrors, others opt to turn a blind eye, posing concerns about accountability and the costs of inaction.

Banality of Evil: Drawing on Hannah Arendt's notion, the film depicts offenders as people capable of both good and evil. Höss' deceptively regular character, compared with his horrible activities, calls into question the simple classification of evil and pushes viewers to face the possibility that it exists inside anybody.

Character Analysis: Rudolf Höss and Those Around Him

The film provides realistic representations of numerous persons stuck beneath the moral abyss of Auschwitz.

Rudolf Höss: The film's principal character is portrayed in a complicated manner. He is shown as a nice family guy and apparently capable leader, despite being responsible for millions of deaths. This juxtaposition pushes the spectator to confront the difficult truth that evil may frequently take on a familiar appearance.

Hedwig Höss (Sandra Hüller): Höss's wife loves the trappings of their wealthy existence while apparently indifferent to the horrors unfolding beyond their door. Her character calls into question the ethics of profiting from unfair institutions, as well as the perils of willful blindness.

Thomas Wünsche is a young SS officer who has a crisis of conscience after learning the truth about the camp. His struggle reflects the internal problems experienced by several Holocaust survivors, urging viewers to ponder the intricacies of human decisions and the possibility of transformation.

The Sonderkommando: These Jewish inmates forced to work in crematoria depict the victims of the Holocaust and the system's degrading effects. Their quiet presence elicits empathy and acts as a continual reminder of the human cost of the horrors.

The Zone of Interest provides a multifaceted examination of the Holocaust and its lasting impact by exploring these characters' perspectives and navigating moral gray areas, leaving viewers to reflect on the complexities of human behavior and the dangers of complacency in the face of injustice.

Printed in Great Britain
by Amazon